D1173491

Cloister Books are inspired by
the monastic custom of walking
slowly and reading or meditating
in the monastery cloister, a place
of silence, centering, and calm.
Within these pages you will find a
similar space in which to pray and
reflect on the presence of God.

Christ's Passion, Our Passions

Christ's Passion, Our Passions

Reflections on the
Seven Last Words from the Cross

Margaret Bullitt-Jonas

Cowley Publications
Cambridge, Massachusetts

Published in the United States of America by Cowley Publications,
a division of the Society of Saint John the Evangelist. No portion of
this book may be reproduced, stored in or introduced into a retrieval
system, or transmitted, in any form or by any means—including
photocopying—without the prior written permission of Cowley
Publications, except in the case of brief quotations embedded in crit-
ical articles and reviews.

Library of Congress Cataloging-in-Publication Data:
Bullitt-Jonas, Margaret.
    Christ's passion, our passions : reflections on the seven last words
from the cross / Margaret Bullitt-Jonas.
        p. cm.
Includes bibliographical references.
    ISBN 1-56101-211-4 (alk. paper)
    1. Jesus Christ—Seven last words—Meditations.   I. Title.

BT457 .B85 2002
232.96'35—dc21

2002155696

Scripture quotations are taken from the following:
New Revised Standard Version of the Bible, © 1989, Division of
Christian Education of the National Council of the Churches of Christ
in the United States of America. Used by permission. All rights reserved.

Revised Standard Version of the Bible, © 1952 (2nd edition, 1971)
by the Division of Christian Education of the National Council of the
Churches of Christ in the United States of America. Used by permission. All rights reserved.

King James Version of the Bible.

Cover design: Gary Ragaglia

This book was printed in the United States of America on acid-free
paper.

Cowley Publications
907 Massachusetts Avenue
Cambridge, Massachusetts 02139
800-225-1534 • www.cowley.org

CONTENTS

ACKNOWLEDGMENTS

This book was conceived in prayer and first delivered as a series of sermons. I am grateful to everyone who participated in the Good Friday service that was held at the Cathedral Church of St. Paul on March 29, 2002. I am indebted to the Dean of the Cathedral, John P. (Jep) Streit, who invited me to preach and suggested the sermons' collective title, and to the Cathedral's Organist and Director of Music, Mark T. Engelhardt, who skillfully shaped the service's flow of music, words, and silence. I want to thank my bishop, M. Thomas Shaw SSJE, for his warm response to the sermons and his suggestion that I offer them to Cowley Publications. Several friends and colleagues helped track down elusive facts: Nora Gallagher, Richard McCall, and my sister, Sister John Marie Bullitt, R.S.M. My agent, Beth Vesel, and her assistant, Emilie Stewart, were staunch allies. It was a pleasure and privilege to work with Kevin R. Hackett SSJE, a first-rate editor and a man of prayer.

For spiritual friendship along the way, thanks go to Nora Gallagher, Deborah Whiting Little, Ruth Redington, Janet Ruffing, R.S.M., Martin L. Smith, and to my mother, Sarah Doering, my brother, John Bullitt, and my sister, Sister John Marie Bullitt, R.S.M.

I am especially grateful to my son Sam and my husband, Robert A. Jonas, who endured the white-hot intensity with which these sermons were written during the course of Holy Week. My husband not only gave tireless and invaluable help as I wrestled with the intricacies of good theology and good writing—he also played *shakuhachi* at the Good Friday worship service. Through his end-blown Japanese flute, Jonas offered us an opportunity to be drawn into the mystery of the Holy One who transcends all words, however eloquently expressed.

Margaret Bullitt-Jonas
ADVENT, 2002

INTRODUCTION

When someone we love is dying, we hang on every word. Is there something she needs? A secret he wants to disclose or some final message she wants to make? Often we probe these last words for years to come, pondering their meaning, struggling sometimes to come to terms with words uttered in anger, despair, or surprise. I'm told that the most common last word of someone about to die from sudden accident or violence is a familiar expletive. Sometimes a person's last words are more ambiguous. Shortly before his death, Goethe reportedly said, "More light!" Was he registering a desire for wisdom, fear of the gathering darkness, or the sight of unexpected radiance? Sometimes a person's last words are unambiguously serene. The last thing Beethoven said before he died was "I shall hear in heaven."

For generations, Christians have gathered at the cross of Christ to ponder his last words. We can probe Christ's words in the same way we sometimes decipher the last words of our loved ones, testing their meaning, wondering what he intended to communicate. But we can also turn the exercise around, for in the end we come to the cross not to probe Christ's words but to let them probe us—to let them work on our minds and hearts as we take our next step toward union with God.

The seven last "words" of Jesus—the seven sentences that the Gospels record Jesus saying from the cross before he died—have captured the imaginations of preachers and writers since at least 1618, when Cardinal Robert Bellarmine published *The Seven Last Words Uttered by Christ on the Cross.* They have inspired composers such as Heinrich Schütz, Franz Joseph Haydn, Theodore Dubois, and more recently James McMillan. They have nourished the personal meditation and prayer of countless seekers through the ages. And for more than three hundred years, Christians have gathered on Good Friday from noon until 3:00 PM to ponder them anew in a service that includes seven sermons, one for each word, interspersed with periods of silence, music, hymns, and prayer. The so-called "Three Hours' Service" was instituted by the Jesuits following an earthquake at Lima in 1687, and was apparently introduced in the Church of England in the 1860s by the Rev. Alexander H. Mackonochie.[1] In both Roman Catholic and Anglican traditions, this devotion developed alongside the Proper Liturgy for Good Friday, which includes lessons and prayers, a ceremonial veneration of the cross, and Holy Communion from bread and wine consecrated the day before.

This book is based on the seven meditations that I preached on Good Friday, 2002, at the Cathedral Church of St. Paul in Boston, Massachusetts. Although I have edited and added material, I have made no effort to change the essential flavor of the words I spoke on the occasion for which they were originally intended. The congregation that gathered on that Good Friday shared an unusual sense of spiritual focus and urgency. This was the first Good Friday since September 11, a personal and national "earthquake" that shook us as decisively as the 1687 upheaval in Lima must have shaken the Jesuits. Like them, we needed to turn to the cross. We needed to draw close to Jesus, to listen to his words, to watch his actions, and to sense, if we could, the spiritual power that was released so many years ago at Golgotha and that continues to reverberate at the center of our lives.

Times of trouble and loss often intensify our search for God, and the quest for God eventually leads every Christian to the cross. The place where the Crucified One spoke his last words and breathed his last breath is the place where suffering and evil are met squarely by the love of God. At the foot of the cross we don't need to pretend that our suffering is not real. Nor need we fear that our suffering will overwhelm us. Because the cross is planted before us, we can finally open ourselves to the reality of suffering and evil: Here all suffering and evil are touched by Love. Here, through the grace of God, all suffering and evil are endured, absorbed, and transformed. Like a lightning rod, the cross of Christ draws all suffering and evil to itself and, neutralizing their power, "grounds" them in Love.

The cross addresses each of us in distinctive ways. At the beginning of each chapter, the "word" appears, along with a full citation locating it in the Gospel's larger story of the Passion. At the end of each chapter, I have provided several questions for reflection and prayer. I suggest that you consider no more than one or two of them at a time. If you tackle them all at once, you are likely to get spiritual indigestion! You may also find it helpful to pray with the biblical passage upon which each chapter is based and with the cross itself. Below I have sketched three approaches to such prayer.

Just as we can never exhaust the love of God, so there are always new riches to discover as we bring to the cross our fears and hopes, our losses and longing. In this book I share some of the insights that have come to me as I have pondered Jesus' last words. My hope is that the Holy Spirit will use these reflections to elicit your own insights and to draw you more deeply into the heart of God, that place of compassion that Jesus disclosed by his words and action from the cross.

Ignatian Contemplation

This mode of prayer is a process of active imagination that was developed by Ignatius of Loyola (1491 or 1495–1556), the founder of the Jesuits.[2] By inviting us to become full participants in a biblical scene, this form of prayer engages many dimensions of the self—feelings, will, memory, and imagination. Do not be concerned about historical accuracy or getting details "right." Do not try to control or analyze what happens as you pray, but simply allow the images to unfold. The imagination can be a powerful doorway to God.

～ Find a comfortable position in which you can be both relaxed and alert. Close your eyes. Take a few deep breaths to release any tension in your body. Then let the breath return to its normal rhythm.

～ Ask God to touch you through the words and actions of the biblical passage you have chosen. As you begin your prayer, what do you desire?

～ Slowly read through the passage once or twice. Pause to notice details and your initial questions, insights, and response.

～ Set the text aside and close your eyes. In your mind's eye, bring the scene to life using all your senses. Allow yourself to become a full participant in the drama that is unfolding before you. What do you see, hear, and smell?

∼ In facing the Crucifixion, what has drawn you to Golgotha? Why are you here? Are you one of the disciples? One of the bystanders? A soldier? Someone in need of healing? Where are you standing in relation to the cross?

∼ What do you notice about Jesus? What do you see and hear when he speaks? How do his words affect the people nearby? How do they affect you?

∼ You may want to talk to Jesus about your feelings. What do you want to ask for? For what do you want to give thanks? What is God trying to show you about yourself? About God?

Lectio Divina

Lectio divina (Latin, sacred reading) can be traced back to the 4th and 5th centuries and is closely associated with St. Benedict and Benedictine spirituality. It involves four steps: *lectio*, *meditatio*, *oratio*, and *contemplatio*, which can be translated as: reading, reflection, response, and rest (or release). There is no need to be rigid in following the order of these steps—for example, you may find yourself moving back and forth between reflecting and responding. That is fine. Trust the process (and the Spirit!). Let the Spirit lead.

~ Find a comfortable position in which you can be both relaxed and alert. Close your eyes. Take a few deep breaths to release any tension in your body. Then let the breath return to its normal rhythm.

~ Ask God to touch you through the biblical passage you have chosen. As you begin your prayer, what do you desire?

LECTIO

~ If possible, read the passage aloud, attentively and reflectively, until a word or phrase catches your imagination or evokes a response. At that moment, pause, put the text aside, and give yourself to prayer. Note: Each step may last only a moment, or may extend over several minutes.

MEDITATIO

~ Gently repeat the word or phrase over and over. Mull on it. Reflect on its meaning. Let the words sink into your heart and mind. Chew on them, as a cow chews its cud. Savor and relish them.

ORATIO

∽ When you feel saturated, share your feelings with the Holy One in whose presence you are. As you take in the insights you received during the "meditatio," what is your spontaneous emotional response? Share your responses with God. Listen. Share.

CONTEMPLATIO

∽ Quietly rest in God's presence. You are lovingly present to one another.

If you get distracted, pick up the text again and resume reading as before, until another word or phrase draws your attention or touches your heart. Continue this peaceful rhythm of reading and pausing. There is no hurry.

Grounding in the Cross

The name I have given to this form of prayer is based on an ancient Tibetan method of developing compassion, as presented by Joanna Macy.[3] I have found it to be a powerful spiritual practice useful not only in solitary prayer and in guided meditation with a group, but also as a way of "breathing through" bad news. I sometimes use it while reading the newspaper or when sitting with someone who is in pain—whenever I need to ground myself again in the strength and love of God. Much of the language, as well as the practices described below are taken from Macy's article, "Despair and Empowerment Work."

∼ Find a comfortable position in which you can be both relaxed and alert. Close your eyes. Take a few deep breaths to release any tension in your body. Then let the breath return to its normal rhythm.

∼ Let your breath bring you an image of the cross of Christ. It may be in front of you, beside or behind you. Sense its weight, its placement deep in the ground. Its roots go deep into the earth, deep into all the muck and mess and pain of human life. Its top lifts high into the sky. It stretches far above you.

∾ Sense the presence of Christ upon the cross. Here is the place where heaven and earth are joined. Here is the place where suffering and evil are lifted up and met by the love of God. Sense the holy power that is near you.

∾ Relax. Become aware of your breathing. As you breathe in, visualize your breath as a stream flowing through your nose, down your windpipe, and into your lungs and heart. As you breathe out, visualize the breath-stream passing through your heart and out into the cross of Christ.

∾ Now open your awareness to the suffering that is present in the world. Drop for now all defenses and open to your knowledge of that suffering. Let it come as concretely as you can, as specific images of your fellow beings in pain, fear, and need. You don't have to strain for these images, for they are already in you because of our interconnectedness. Relax and let them surface, breathing them in, breathing them through to the cross of Christ.

∾ Breathe in the pain like a dark stream, up

through your nose, down into your lungs and heart, and out into the cross of Christ. All you need to do is let it pass through your heart and into the cross.

～ Keep breathing. Be sure that the stream flows through and out again. Don't hang on to the pain. Surrender it for now to the healing power of Christ.

～ If you need to weep, that is all right. Release the tears. When our hearts break open to the sufferings of the world, we enter the heart of Christ. The heart that breaks open can contain the whole universe. Your heart—Christ's heart—is that large. Trust it. Keep breathing.

1 "Three Hours' Service, The" in *The Oxford Dictionary of the Christian Church,,* 2nd ed. ed. by F. L. Cross and E. A. Livingstone (Oxford: Oxford University Press, 1983), p. 1375.

2 For a fine account of Ignatian contemplation, *lectio divina*, and other ways to pray, see Martin L. Smith, *The Word Is Very Near You: A Guide to Praying with Scripture* (Cambridge, MA: Cowley Publications, 1989).

3 Joanna Rogers Macy, "Despair and Empowerment Work," in *Living with Apocalypse: Spiritual Resources for Social Compassion*, ed. Tilden H. Edwards (San Francisco: Harper & Row, 1984), pp. 126–127. Several sentences are taken verbatim (e.g. "Now open your awareness . . . as concretely as you can," "The heart that breaks open . . . ," and "Trust it. Keep breathing."). "Grounding in the Cross" is presented in my article, "Feeling and Pain and Prayer," first published in *Review for Religious* Vol. 54, No. 3 (May–June), 1995: pp. 433–446, and reprinted in the anthology Praying as a Christian, *The Best of the Review* (7), ed.David L. Fleming, S.J. (St. Louis, MO: *Review for Religious*, 2000) pp. 139–152.

ONE

Father, forgive them
for they know not what they do.

(LUKE 23:32–38)

This is the first Good Friday since the terror unleashed on September 11. If we were once lulled by the soothing fantasy that terrorism couldn't touch us and that life was basically predictable and safe, now we have been startled awake. Violence has become real to us again. The images that have always confronted us through newspapers and television and that once might have generated no more than a shrug or a sigh, now snag our attention. Another suicide bombing in Israel. An Afghani soldier dragged out of a ditch and into the center of the road, pleading in vain for his life. A man's body thrown over that of his infant grandson in a futile attempt to prevent the baby from breathing toxic gas.

The reality of violence presses upon us in other ways. We are acutely aware of the violence being done not only to other human beings but also to the natural world. Scientists warn that if we don't sharply reduce the rate at which we burn fossil fuels, global warming could raise worldwide average temperatures between three and eleven degrees Fahrenheit within this century. Sea levels are already rising. The deep oceans are heating. Tundra is thawing. Ice in the Arctic has thinned forty per cent in the last forty years. Climate instability is causing increasingly violent weather, with intense hurricanes or floods in some parts of the world and increased drought in others. Birds are migrating. Ecosystems are shifting. Environmental refugees are on the move. In one small but telling example of the effects of global warming, because there was no ice last winter in the Gulf of St. Lawrence, harp seals were forced to give birth to their pups in the open water, where they drowned.[1]

Climate change, the extinction of species, terrorism, war—the challenges that presently face the human community can seem overwhelming. Each of us also carries the burden of our own personal pain, our private losses and disappointment, whatever worry, grief, or anger is secretly gnawing at our heart. Such personal and collective suffering is more than we alone can bear. What are we to do with this pain? Where can we go?

We go to the cross. The cross of Christ is the place where the suffering and evil of the world are met by God's infinite compassion and mercy. "Father, forgive them for they know not what they do." These words of Christ are not just spoken once. They are spoken again and again, as the form of the Greek verb (*elegen*) makes clear: Jesus *kept* saying, "Father, forgive them."

We need those words more than ever this year. We need to bring our pain to Christ, to express it, to offer it, and to let it be met by his love. Luke's Gospel is sometimes called "the Gospel of the great pardons," and we desperately need that Gospel pardon today. We need to take it into our hearts again and again, as often as we want to, as often as we need to. We need the loving-kindness and forgiveness of a God who loves us to the end.

Yet when we hear this first word from the cross,

something in us may want to protest. In a more innocent, peaceful time, listening to Jesus say "Father, forgive them" might be easy to dismiss as rather sweet—an admirable sentiment, though somewhat naive. But in times of conflict and pain—such as the one in which Jesus lived, or the one in which we live now—we experience the full impact of these words. They strike us as shocking, even outrageous. "Don't talk to me about forgiveness!" something in us wants to shout. "If you hit me, I'll hit you back!" Why should we forgive someone who has inflicted an injury on us or someone we love? What does it mean to forgive a terrorist or sociopath or serial killer? Does it mean condoning rape or child abuse? Does it mean refusing to defend oneself and allowing oneself to be treated like a doormat? There are times when talk of forgiveness is glib and cheap, a way of ignoring or even colluding with evil.

The word "forgiveness" is as elusive as the word "God"—and as open to distortion and misinterpretation. But the cycle of retaliation prowls the world, "threatening to devour it" (1 Peter 5:8), and in these precarious times we need urgently to explore what authentic forgiveness really means. It's a mistake to think that forgiveness has no future, for, in the stark words of Archbishop Desmond Tutu, there is "no future without forgiveness."[2]

We can't will our way to genuine forgiveness. We can only find our way. And to do that we undertake a voyage as risky as the one Odysseus took between Scylla and Charybdis. Maybe you remember the story from the *Odyssey*, Homer's epic describing the adventures of Odysseus on his twenty-year voyage home from Troy. One of the most daunting challenges he faces is how to pass through a narrow strait. On one side is a tall mountain with sheer cliffs of polished stone, home of the mythical monster Scylla, which seizes ships that comes near and devours as many sailors as it can. On the other side of the strait is a dangerous whirlpool that harbors the monster Charybdis, ready at any moment to suck a passing ship into the depths of the sea. Odysseus is in a treacherous situation: If he navigates his ship away from one threat, he may fall prey to the other. Yet the only way forward is to make his way through the strait.

We too face twin dangers as we try to navigate our hearts in the direction of forgiveness. When we are badly hurt, we can become like Scylla, as stony as a mountain, self-righteously announcing, "I will *never* forgive you, no matter what!" Or, filled with secret rage, we may offer a bogus forgiveness. The phrase "I forgive you," uttered from the cold heights of pride, can carry the force of a slap. This kind of "forgiveness" is not forgiveness at all—it is really just another act of aggression.

There's nothing inherently wrong with anger. It's natural to be angry when we've been hurt. But when we hang on to anger, nursing it along, letting it become so familiar—even necessary—to our sense of self that we can't let it go, then some corner of our heart becomes hard and embittered, a cold, stony rock in the middle of the ocean, sheltering a monster.

In order not to get trapped in that perpetually angry, embittered place, we may swing instead to the opposite extreme, plunging straight into the whirlpool of Charybdis. This is what happens when we shrug off our anger and decide that the injury doesn't matter. "Oh, it's nothing. I don't mind," we may say. "Of course, I forgive you." And then we put on a happy face and go on with our lives, pretending, as best we can, that nothing happened. We try to convince ourselves—and God—that we feel loving, peaceful, and forgiving. Like a whirlpool in the ocean, we swallow the anger, swallow the hurt, and assume it's gone.

But of course it's not. The body registers and stores the memories and feelings we suppress. We may spend a lot of energy trying to push them out of our awareness. We may work hard to keep our minds dulled or busy. We may avoid the quiet of prayer and the possibility that some long-feared truth will swim into consciousness, like a fish that only surfaces when the lake is still. But one way or another, what we repress will try to make itself known. Tense and restless, we may find ourselves kicking the dog, developing an ulcer, or being haunted by bad dreams, until, by God's grace, we finally face the truth we have repressed; "For there is nothing hidden, except to be disclosed; nor is anything secret, except to come to light" (Mark 4:22).

The fact is, when we are hurt, we do feel anger, sorrow, and pain. To pretend otherwise is to deny the human condition. If, out of the best Christian motives, we put on a mask of forgiveness and try to act pleasant and make everything nice, we find that we no longer relate to one another as real people. We only show each other our masks. And we wonder why we feel so alienated and lonely.

So, there is the Scylla of unforgiving hard-heartedness, and the Charybdis of an easygoing and bogus forgiveness. How then do we find that narrow path between the two, what Jesus might call the "narrow door" (Luke 13:24), the "narrow gate" (Matthew 7:13), to the kingdom of God? I'd like to offer a few guideposts for the journey.

First, in order to forgive, we must face the damage that has been done. It's no good to minimize and brush off the pain. If we want to forgive, we have to feel and bear the anger, grief, and vulnerability that arise when we've been hurt. Of course we'd prefer to skip this step. It's not pleasant to feel pain or to admit that "Yes, we *do* mind it."

Yet I wonder if Jesus was able, in the midst of his agony on the cross, to say "Father, forgive them, for they know not what they do," because he was also able to cry out, "My God, my God, why have you forsaken me?" Jesus was straightforward with his companions and with God. He wept, he laughed, he got angry, he asked for help, he felt anguish, he let himself be utterly transparent to the One to whom "all hearts are open, all desires known, and from whom no secrets are hid."[3]

Because of that openness with God, that willingness to share his whole self with God—all his feelings, the whole range of human experience— Jesus was able to ground himself in divine compassion. If we want to learn to forgive, we must be willing to make a large space in our prayer time to let ourselves—and God—know the whole range of what we feel. We must resist jumping ahead to what we think we *should* be feeling, but instead explore what is actually in us. Gradually we learn to sit in God's presence with our anger, feeling its heat, or with our sorrow, feeling its waves. Gradually, we learn to wait until we feel something shift, and God shows us what else we need to see.

Second, forgiveness requires honest self-examination. When I'm upset by something that happened, it's tempting to look for a scapegoat. Give me someone, anyone, to blame! But truth requires that I assess my own responsibility. In what way did I contribute to the situation? Am I angry with someone in order to avoid noticing how guilty I feel and how angry I am at myself? Am I outraged by a behavior in someone else that I fail to recognize as my own? Am I projecting my own faults on someone else, blaming him or her for crimes that are also mine? Pulling back our projections is basic to the process of forgiveness, as we learn to accept the fact that the very behaviors we condemn in others may be expressions of parts of ourselves that we despise and fear. Our struggle to forgive someone else may bring us face to face with our own difficulty in forgiving ourselves or accepting God's forgiveness.

The events of September 11 and those following have reminded Americans that whether we like it or not, and whether we know it or not, our country's policies are implicated to some degree in what takes place abroad, for good and for ill. Both as individuals and as a nation, truth requires that we explore how we have contributed to the hatred that many other members of the global community feel toward our country. Self-examination is a stage we can't afford to omit if we want to move toward lasting peace.

Finally, forgiveness depends on prayer. In our prayer we can listen attentively to Jesus praying for us on the cross. We can listen to Jesus' words of forgiveness as we bring before him our greed, pride, and impatience, our guilt and shame. When we stand near the cross, discovering that we are loved to the core, we receive not only the forgiveness we need, we receive the power and courage to forgive others. It is when we realize that we are both sinful and forgiven that the power arises in us to convey forgiveness to others.

And we can go one step further. We can listen to Jesus' words of forgiveness as we bring before him our enemies, those people we most fear and despise. Jesus is constantly interceding not only for us but also for them, pleading that God's love and mercy be at the center of our lives *and* theirs. Can we pray to see our enemies as God sees them? It's not an easy prayer, and you may resist praying it as strenuously as I have. But when I pray to see the other person through the eyes of God, slowly I begin to see that the other person is wounded, hurting, and imperfect, as I am; sinning, as I am; and yet beloved by God, as I am.

This realization changes everything. It affects our behavior and our response. It sets us free from the reflexive urge to pursue revenge, enabling us to look for creative solutions to conflict. It sets us free from hatred, releasing our energy to seek fresh approaches to healing old wounds.

Forgiveness is like a stream that pours out at the center of our being through the power of the cross. We can't force it or grasp it any more than we can hold a river in our fist. But we can pray for it and do what we can to be open to it. And we can accept the fact that forgiveness is almost never a single event but a process.

The three suggestions that I offer—to face and feel our anger and sadness, to examine ourselves honestly, and to pray—have been guideposts in my own journey toward forgiveness. Alongside this inner work, we will surely be led to take action. God may call us to do something outward: to make amends, to offer an apology, to confront a wrong, to look for non-violent ways to stop injustice. But God is always calling us to take inward action, too, to perform, in the secrecy of our own hearts, that invisible and astonishing act through which we share in the divine life: to forgive.

And so we dare to hope that, like Odysseus, we will travel safely between the stony rock of Scylla and the whirlpool of Charybdis, and together, through the narrow gate of Christ, come home at last into the spacious and merciful heart of God.

To Ponder in Prayer . . .

Invite the Holy Spirit to help you examine your heart.

Where are you locked in bitterness, hatred, or resentment? Where have you become as hard as stone? Ask God the Creator for the willingness to let go old resentments. Where are you swallowing anger, sorrow, or fear and pretending that everything is fine?

Ask the Holy Spirit for the courage to admit your suffering.

What is the anger you need to express? What are the tears you need to shed? Where are you holding these feelings in your body? Touch this place with your hand. Are you willing to share them with Jesus? To ask for healing? Ask Christ to embrace you as you experience your anger or sorrow.

Ask Christ to hold whatever is more than you can bear.

For what do you need to ask God's forgiveness? Who are the people you need to forgive? Who are the people from whom you need to seek forgiveness? Listen to Jesus saying: "Father, forgive them." He is praying for you. How do you respond? Listen again to Jesus: "Father, forgive them." He is praying for your enemies. How do you respond?

1 Many recent books provide a readable summary of the science of global climate change, including, for example, *The End of Nature*, by Bill McKibben (New York: Anchor Books, 1999 [10th anniversary edition with a new introduction]) and *The Heat Is On: The Climate Crisis, the Cover-up*, the Prescription, by Ross Gelbspan (Perseus Publishing, 1998). For ongoing information from around the world about global warming, including an archive of more than 20,000 articles written since 1999, visit Climate Ark (www.climateark.org). For ongoing general news about the environment, visit Environmental News Network (www.enn.com/index.asp). For information about the interfaith movement to address global warming, check, for instance, Interfaith Climate Change Network (www.protectingcreation.org), a project of the National Council of Churches of Christ in the USA and the Coalition on the Environment and Jewish Life, and Religious Witness for the Earth (www.religiouswitness.org), an interfaith, activist network dedicated to non-violent public witness in defense of Creation.

2 Desmond Mpilu Tutu, *No Future Without Forgiveness* (New York: Doubleday, 2000).

3 Collect for Purity, *The Book of Common Prayer* (New York: Church Publishing, Inc., 1979) p. 355.

TWO

*Today you will be with me
in Paradise.*

(LUKE 23:19–43)

Luke's account of the crucifixion presents a brutal, messy scene of human conflict. At its center is Jesus, hanging on the cross. The other characters in the scene stand at varying distances from the cross, like rings around a hub. At the outer rim is an anonymous crowd of people, many of whom have probably gathered for this execution—as people still gather today—because they want to watch someone die. Some of them may be as pitiless as voyeurs at a car accident, eager for a thrill. Closer in are the religious leaders who scoff specifically at Jesus, and closer still the jeering

Roman soldiers who offer him sour wine, apparently not to ease his thirst or take the edge off his pain but simply to toy with him. Then we come to the first criminal, the thief crucified on one side of Jesus who mocks him, saying, "Are you not the Messiah? Save yourself and us!"

It's uncomfortable to stay too long in the company of these people, for their bitterness and bile leap from the page. If truth be told, I hear those voices within myself, as well, the voices of violence and retribution, the voices that take satisfaction in someone else's suffering or misfortune. There is a certain malicious pleasure in watching someone else take the hit. And sometimes it's so much fun to ridicule the other guy. If I can laugh at you, then I must be bigger than you are, I must be more important and worthy. If I feel small inside, if I feel anxious or inadequate, I can always puff myself up by finding fault with someone else. And hey, if I feel upset or afraid, why not make someone else feel as frightened as I do? Why not lash out and make others feel the pain that I feel—kind of spread it around?

I know those voices, as perhaps you do, too, so I can identify with everyone in this scene. Some contemptuous voices seem to have a direct pipeline to evil—one of Satan's traditional names is the Accuser. But behind the impulse to hurt someone else, behind the urge to sneer, there often lies a hidden wound in need of healing. The people surrounding Jesus that we've considered so far—the crowds, the religious leaders, the soldiers, the first thief—are all suffering, but we might call it a "closed" suffering. It's the sort of suffering that is locked in on itself and of which we may or may not be entirely conscious. Suffering that is "closed" just perpetuates itself: As individuals and as nations we can endlessly repeat the cycle of hurt and retaliation, and spread the suffering to others, sometimes without meaning to, sometimes with deliberate and conscious malice. The powers of evil work very effectively when we do not open our suffering to the power and mercy of God.

According to all four Gospel accounts of Jesus' death, not everyone who gathered near the cross was closed to God's presence. In Luke's version of the story, a group of sorrowing women who have followed Jesus from Galilee stands watching "at a distance" (Luke 23:49). Luke does not give us the women's names, but their courage is self-evident and their grief and love are clear (Luke 23:27). The women's pain is real, but unlike the hidden pain of the abusive spectators, it has been washed clean of any spite. It is filled with compassion.

How does someone move from the contempt and cruelty of the crowds to the empathy and connection embodied in these women? The transformation of one man's soul—one person's remarkable, last-minute journey from hard-heartedness to compassion—is shown in Luke's account of the second thief, the man who is crucified on Jesus' other side. The story does not explain what triggers the fellow's shift of perception or change of heart. All we know is that although the man is apparently as mixed-up and malicious as everyone else, as he looks at Jesus, something inside him opens. He turns to the first thief and rebukes him, admitting that both he and the other criminal are guilty, and that Jesus is innocent. And then, in a plea that resounds through the centuries, the second thief turns to Jesus and asks, "Jesus, remember me when you come into your kingdom." (Luke 23:43)

This is the prayer of a man who, as death draws near, has seen his long and sordid life flash before his eyes. Turning to Jesus, he asks only to be remembered. "Remember me kindly," he seems to plead. "See what is worthy in me. Love me even if the world proclaims me unlovable."

When we are remembered, we are connected with the ones who hold us in memory; we are restored to union. The opposite of *re*membered might be *dis*membered, torn apart. When we remember someone kindly, when we are remembered kindly, then we're made whole again, and we make each other whole. Only someone who knows what it's like to be forgotten, to feel alienated or estranged, knows the urgent longing to be remembered.

The plea of the penitent thief, his willingness to turn to Jesus to ask for help, is the only opening that Jesus needs. All Jesus needs is the tiniest of signs, the smallest chink in the wall of the man's self-enclosed prison, and, in an instant, Jesus offers him everything, his very self. Over Jesus' head is an inscription, "This is the King of the Jews," but if Jesus is a king, he is a king who yearns to share his glory—a king who gives *us* a crown.

"Today," he says, in a declaration that some have called 'the Gospel within the Gospel,' "today you will be with me in Paradise." It's as if Jesus was turning to the thief with shining eyes to say,

"Come on then! Let's go! From now on we're in this together! I won't leave you behind. I will *never* leave you behind. I will be with you always, and you will share in everything that I receive."

Can you imagine how the thief responds to these words? How do you respond? It is worth exploring this encounter in prayer, for the dialogue between Jesus and the penitent thief is one that takes place within us whenever we turn in hope to Christ, asking for mercy.

Can you imagine what Jesus is experiencing as he utters this promise? Even in the extremity of pain, he extends kindness. Like the two men crucified beside him—like every human being—he is mortal, he is going down, he is being felled by death. And not a painless, peaceful death either, not the calm bedside scene that most of us hope will be *our* lot, but an agonizing and violent end. Yet despite the reality of present pain and imminent death, Jesus holds fast to a greater certainty: Paradise is real. What's more, he knows that this is where he's heading—that paradise, God's dwelling-place, is his destiny, source, and home. And that he will not go to paradise by himself—he intends to bring with him the man who is beside him.

It would be presumptuous to claim that we can fully know for ourselves what was going through Jesus' mind and heart at this moment. Unlike us, he was fully divine, as well as fully human. Still, we are called to have "the mind of Christ" (1 Corinthians 2:16b), and surely there are times in our prayer, and in our lives, when we glimpse something of the truth that Jesus knew as he spoke this word from the cross. There are times, for example, when like Paul we know that our present sufferings "are not worth comparing with the glory about to be revealed to us" (Romans 8:18). There are times in our prayer, and in our lives, when we know that, however vivid the suffering within or around us, we are nonetheless held in God's everlasting arms. There are times in our prayer, and in our lives, when we know that paradise exists not only in the future but also now, hidden in the present. There are times in our prayer, and in our lives, when our deepest desire is to be a blessing to others and we know that our joy will not be complete until others share it, too.

Such moments of insight are like sparks from the same fire, like rays from the same light that shines in Jesus' words, "Today you will be with me in Paradise." Every act of generosity and mercy resonates with this word, and springs from the same source. Perhaps the only thing as joyful as hearing it addressed to us is finding ourselves expressing it to someone else.

Every single person in this scene is a part of ourselves, from the indifferent stranger at the outer ring to the crucified Christ at the hub. In prayer we gradually discover our connection with each of them and allow each part of ourselves—indifferent, vindictive, contemptuous, contrite—to be brought to the cross and there transformed. As we ponder this word of blessing from the cross, we may eventually identify with Christ himself. We may sense within us the spring of living water "gushing up to eternal life" (John 4:14), the perpetual outpouring of mercy that we receive from Christ and that moves through us and out into the world.

The dialogue between the penitent thief and Jesus takes place not only in our solitary prayer, but in every Eucharist, as we turn again with hope to the One who lived, died, and rose for us. Like the penitent thief, we come to the Eucharist in part to plead, "Remember me." And at the Eucharist, our longing for Jesus to remember us meets Jesus' longing that we remember him. "Do this," he told us, and tells us still, "in remembrance of me." As we open our hands to receive Christ's body in the bread and the wine, as we open our minds and hearts to receive his presence, we remember him and he remembers us, and so we are made whole.

To Ponder in Prayer . . .

If Jesus were beside you now, gazing with compassion on your suffering and the mess that you—like all of us—have sometimes made of things, what would you say to him? What happens as you share this with him? How does he respond?

Is there a secret you want or need to confess to him, a longing for wholeness, a desire to be remembered kindly? What do you need to express, so that you, too, can open to that intimate life with him that we call paradise? How does he respond?

Perhaps you know the musical setting by Jacques Berthier, written for the Taizé Community, "Jesus, remember me when you come into your kingdom." Practice singing this slowly as you pray for yourself, then let it become an intercessory prayer: As you sing, bring to mind one by one all those who long for healing and mercy, all those who long to be set free. Let yourself sing not only for the people you know, but also for those in other cities, countries, and continents. Let the circle of prayer grow very large. Take up the song of all Creation—of every wolf and warbler, snake and salmon—as it "waits with eager longing" (Romans 8:19) for fulfillment.

Jesus promises to be with us in paradise—not at some future date, not just after we die, but today, at this very moment. Take some time to sit with Jesus in silence, bringing awareness to your breath and letting your thoughts and feelings grow quiet. Can you sense the paradise that he is offering you?

St. Athanasius, one of the early Church Fathers, advised, "Always breathe Christ." Breathe in the loving kindness that Jesus is extending to you right now. Breathe out that loving kindness to every person or concern that comes to mind. Breathe in Christ's loving kindness, letting it stream through every cell of your body. Breathe it out, freely passing it on—there's no need to hoard. With every breath, give away the paradise that is perpetually being given to you.

THREE

Woman, behold your son.
Son, behold your mother.

(JOHN 19:23–27)

Standing near the cross of Jesus are some of his dearest family members and friends. In a gesture that expresses the reconciling power of the cross, Jesus now gives Mary, his mother, to the beloved disciple and the beloved disciple to Mary. "Woman," he says gently, "here is your son . . . here is your mother."[1] However close the two of them may have been until this moment, from now on Christ has drawn them into a fuller, more intimate, and more conscious connection with each other than they had before.

How much we matter to each other! How

much we need each other! "Only connect." Those are the well-known words of novelist E. M. Forster[2], and in a world of broken relationships, loneliness, and lovelessness, how hungry we are to have people in our lives who know us through and through and who love us as we really are. Within each person there is a "yearning man" or "yearning woman," a secret part of ourselves that longs to know and be known, to encounter and be encountered in an authentic way.

We may yearn for belonging, but there are also energies within and around us that conspire to lead us anywhere but toward authentic friendship and community. We all know the myriad ways to avoid human relationship. We can dive into the next drink, grab another handful of cookies, or plunge into overwork. Feeling a little anxious or bored? Go shopping. Loneliness getting to you? Find some pornography on the Internet. Or study celebrities in a cheap, tabloid magazine—scrutinize their lovers, their income, their clothes; shake your head at the latest scandals. Feeling sad or stressed? Take the edge off by numbing out in front of the TV set. In short, do something—*anything*—rather than risk sharing our real selves with those close to us and admitting the truth of our deep need to connect.

I recently read a wonderful book by Bill Mc-Kibben, *The Age of Missing Information*, and he points out that not too long ago a court in Finland ordered McDonald's to take an advertisement off the air. The commercial "showed a boy who was sad about moving to a new home until he saw a Golden Arches across the street. This, the court ruled, 'falsely leads people to believe that a Big Mac can replace friends and ease loneliness.'"[3] The court was on to something, because of course that's the big lie: That our heart's longing for connection can be satisfied by "stuff." That a Big Mac can do it. That watching reruns can do it. That fame can do it. That winning can do it. That a big house, a big car, a big bank account can do it.

Into the lie of alienation and estrangement bursts the cross of Christ, shattering the lie, and unmasking the illusion. So much for golden arches! The vertical pole of the cross restores the union of heaven and earth, and Christ's outstretched arms gather together all creatures on earth, human and other-than-human alike. "Woman," Jesus says to us, "here is your son. Here is your mother." In his outpouring love on the cross, Jesus not only gives us himself, he gives us back to each other—across genders, across generations—restoring connection among all human beings, those near to us and those who are far away.

We know this for ourselves in the interactions that weave the tapestry of our daily lives. In the heat of a fight with a family member or friend, for instance, pausing to pray can open a fresh perspective. When a stinging word is on the tip of my tongue and everything in me is poised for the kill, it can be startling to recall the presence of the crucified Christ who loves me utterly, and who (even more surprisingly) utterly loves my impossible family member, too. At the foot of the cross, how pointless—even shameful—it suddenly seems to be locked in brutal combat. And so, by the grace of God, I can lay down the verbal hand grenade and look with new eyes at my combatant: this is the very person whom Jesus has given me to love; there must be a better way to resolve our differences.

Conversely, the more clearly we perceive Jesus' longing to create communities of mutual belonging and affection, the more likely we'll feel challenged to disrupt family or collegial patterns of withdrawal, cut-off, and isolation. When I am tempted to give someone the silent treatment or the cold shoulder, how chastening (and enlightening) it becomes to return to the cross. Like it or not, Jesus lived, died, and rose again as much for the other guy as for me. In fact, his risen presence—and his dying words—call into being a community of love in which no one is first and no one is last, no one is left out and no one is left behind.

There is no ready-made formula for the costly, risky work of human connection. Sometimes the way to move forward is to speak up; sometimes it is to listen. Sometimes the way to real intimacy is to ditch the habit of conflict and our familiar taunt or complaint; at other times we must move past avoidance and stop settling for being "nice," stop "going along to get along." We each must make our own mistakes as we learn when to speak and when to keep silent, when to reach out and when to wait.

Learning to love well takes patience and discernment. It takes discipline, too. Staying inwardly close to the cross is a wise place to stay, for it is here that God's love in Christ is perpetually poured out and community is always being formed. With Jesus' words from the cross ringing in our ears, we find the courage and the will to do what we can to honor the people he is giving us to love. And, when we are disappointed or frustrated in our human relationships, it is to the cross that we can return, as we rest in the certainty of Christ's love.

The love that pours from the cross extends not only to our small circle of family members and friends but to everyone. It may be a cliché to say that we are all one family, but when we touch this truth for ourselves it changes our perception forever. I remember a cold winter morning ten years ago, not long after the death of my daughter, Rebecca.[4] She was our second child and perfect in every way, but she was born two months too soon. After a four-hour ordeal in intensive care, during which her tiny arms were spread wide so that monitors, needles, and tubes could be affixed to her body, my husband and I finally consented to stop heroic medical intervention. We gently removed Rebecca from her cross, and she died quietly in our arms.

I have never felt, neither before nor since, a loss as pure or a sorrow as deep. Desperate for an extended period of prayer, I decided to spend a few days at a retreat house on the seacoast north of Boston. On a cold winter morning I found myself sitting in the dining hall and weeping into my coffee as I watched the waves of the Atlantic rise and crest and fall. It occurred to me that Rebecca's life, like that of every mortal, was as transient as a wave. What could I do with the passionate love that had been released with her birth and death? It seemed I had three choices.

I could cling fiercely to the small "wave" that was Rebecca and refuse to let her go. I could hang on tight and drown myself in bitterness and anger.

A second possibility was to remove myself entirely from such ardent personal love and mildly try to love the ocean as a whole. I could strive for stoic indifference and coolly love humanity from afar. I could try to refrain from loving any waves in particular.

A third possibility—the insight that broke open my heart—was that I could love all the waves with the love that I'd known in this one wave. Maybe Rebecca was my doorway to perceiving the preciousness of every person. Maybe the fervent love that I felt for this one small child was a glimpse into the love that God holds for each one of us.

The stranger leaning impatiently over the steering wheel as he hurtles past me on the highway:

He is loved by God as I loved and still love Rebecca. The white-haired lady choosing toothpaste at the drug store, the neighbor walking his black lab, the weary postal clerk who hardly says hello, the parishioner who gives away home-grown tomatoes in the parish hall, even the telemarketer interrupting our dinner to make a pitch for a magazine subscription: each is loved by God as I love Rebecca. "Behold your daughter," says a voice within me as I gaze at them. Through the cross of Christ, the love I feel for my daughter is everywhere I look. It belongs to everyone.

And there is more. Jesus gave his life to reconcile human beings not only with one another and with God but with the whole creation. We don't hear about this very much, for since the Reformation, the Western Church has been preoccupied with human salvation and underplayed the salvation of the natural world and the entire cosmos. But in a period of human history in which the natural world is under prolonged assault, when the climate's stability is at risk, when hundreds of plant and animal species just within the United States are threatened or endangered,[5] when natural resources are being consumed at an accelerating rate and we are soon to reach the limits of what this planet can sustain, the time has come to restore the wholeness of the faith. We need to reclaim the early Church's understanding that Jesus died not only for human beings, but for all creation. Life in its totality—not just human life—has been reconciled, restored, and transformed through the power of the cross.

When Jesus says, "Behold your mother," perhaps he is inviting us to cherish Mary not only as the Queen of heaven, but as the natural mother of Jesus, the sign of our rootedness in this good earth. Among some indigenous peoples, Mary symbolizes the ancient Corn Mother, and perhaps for us she can symbolize Mother Earth. We could say that with this word, Jesus is giving human beings and nature back to one another in a relationship of mutual care and interdependence. Jesus is asking the beloved disciple, who stands for all people, to take Mary into his house, which means into his heart and under his protection. True reconciliation between humanity and nature means the reverse, as well: as humans we take our place in nature's "house," recognizing that we belong to a web of life upon which we depend and whose "house rules" we violate at our peril.

The love that Jesus released on the cross flows out in all directions, revealing our connections with one another, with God, and with all creation. If we practice staying inwardly near the cross, we will gradually be drawn into a process of spiritual transformation through which our consciousness is changed. We will take on the mind of Christ and perceive these inter-connections ourselves.

To Ponder in Prayer . . .

"Behold your mother. Behold your son." These words resonate within us, raising questions that we alone can answer. Do I in fact behold the other person with loving eyes? Do I honestly long for genuine connection? If not, why not? Am I willing to speak to Jesus about this, and to ask for his healing and probing word? If I feel Jesus nudging me to initiate, restore, or renew a particular relationship, what is the most authentic way to do so?

As you go through the day, bring to mind this word from the cross. Listen to these words as you interact with other people—as you wait in line, as you drive, as you pick up the phone, as you talk to a family member or friend. Listen to these words as you interact with the natural world—as you feel a breeze on your face, as you catch sight of a tree, as you sense the earth beneath your feet. What happens? How do you respond? What are the relationships that Jesus is inviting you to explore, reclaim, or redeem?

Go outside for a contemplative walk. Walk slowly and in silence, letting each step draw you into the present moment. Notice sounds, smells, and colors. If you feel drawn to do so, invite Christ to walk beside you.

Let some part of the natural world draw your attention. Pause to spend time with it. Use all your senses. Engage your body, if you can: touch the object, sit down on it if it is a rock, lean against it. Maybe you have seen it a thousand times before, but see it today as if for the first time. Notice every detail, pondering it quietly. Let what you are gazing at disclose itself to you. Let God be present in your gazing.

How is God addressing you through the natural world? What is God trying to show you? How do you respond?

1 I am using interchangeably two different translations of the same verse from the Gospel of John, "Behold" (*King James Version, Revised Standard Version*) and "Here is" (*New Revised Standard Version*).

2 E. M. Forster, epigraph to *Howard's End*, (New York: Penguin Books, 1992), p. 148.

3 Bill McKibben, *The Age of Missing Information*, (New York: Penguin, 1992, Plume, 1993), p. 122.

4 The following story is more fully elaborated in my article, "Even at the Grave We Make Our Song," *Review for Religious* 53 (May–June 1994): pp. 420–435. See also: Robert A. Jonas, *Rebecca: A Father's Journey from Grief to Gratitude*, (New York: Crossroad, 1995).

5 U.S. Fish and Wildlife Service, Endangered Species Information, http://endangered.fws.gov/wildlife.html#Species.

FOUR

My God, my God,
why have you forsaken me?

(Matthew 27:45–49)

In 1942, German troops invaded the city of Stalingrad, beginning one of the most ferocious battles of World War II. A commentator reports that within months, the German Sixth Army was "entirely cut off from help and abandoned to perish. The final plane out of the city carried seven bags of mail, and among those were the last letters written by the German soldiers who were, at that point, freezing, starving, and facing death."[1]

One of those desperate soldiers wrote a letter home to his pastor:

. . . In Stalingrad, to put the question of God's existence means to deny it. . . . I regret my words. . . . because they will be my last, and I won't be able to speak any other words afterwards which might reconcile you and make up for these.

You are a pastor, Father, and in one's last letter one says only what is true or what one believes might be true. I have searched for God in every crater, in every destroyed house, on every corner, in every friend, in my foxhole, and in the sky. God did not show Himself, even though my heart cried for Him. . . . on earth there was hunger and murder, from the sky came bombs and fire, only God was not there. No, Father, there is no God. Again I write it and know that this is terrible and I cannot make up for it ever. And if there should be a God, He is only with you in the hymnals and prayers, in the pious sayings of the priests and pastors, in the ringing of the bells and the fragrance of incense, but not in Stalingrad.[2]

Not in Stalingrad. Not in the furthest reaches of human despair. Not in the emptiness of Jesus' anguish on the cross. "My God, my God, why have you forsaken me?"

Some biblical scholars try to muffle the horror

of this moment. Jesus doesn't really mean it, they say; he is just quoting a psalm; he only wants to show that scripture is being fulfilled; he recites the psalm's terrible first line only because he knows it ends in joy. Unlikely. I believe that Jesus is actually experiencing the depth of human anguish. His cry is genuine. He speaks here in his native Aramaic, because in deep distress we all revert to our native tongue. Like the soldier in Stalingrad—like many of us in our most desperate hour—he is experiencing complete interior abandonment.

What does this mean? For one thing, a faith that believes that God will not let us suffer is not a Gospel faith. Surely the sight of Jesus enduring the deepest suffering a human being can know should burn away any fond hope that a faithful journey into God will keep us safe from hardship or distress.

The way to resurrection is through the experience of a pain and dying that cannot be bypassed. Your crucifixion and mine will be different. There are innumerable ways that human beings finally reach their cross. Maybe what we've long feared has come true: Our mother has Alzheimer's or our son is doing drugs. Maybe there's no money for the rent, or we've been stranded in the same dull job for years and probably won't find something better. Maybe we've never found the life partner we've always longed for. Maybe we're stuck in bitterness or blame, in envy or resentment.

One way or another, all of us learn that in our life with God there comes a time when the only way to new life is by enduring and accepting a blinding bolt of pain that breaks everything apart. There was nothing sentimental about Jesus' Good Friday, and there is nothing sentimental about our own, either. Nothing sweetly melancholy, nothing faintly indulgent—as though we were slumming for a day before we hurry back in relief to the comfort of our ordinary lives. When we reach our Good Friday, we are confronted starkly with death, for in every crucifixion there is a death we need to die.

My own first crucifixion came over 20 years ago. On Good Friday in 1982, after a lifetime of addiction, I made my way back to church and faced the fact that my entire life was a lie. I needed to die to a whole way of being. What needed to die? My numbness needed to die. The hard shell around me had to crack open at last and drop away. My denial needed to die, the pretense that everything was fine and that suffering and death were not real. My despair needed to die, the lie that suffering and death have the last word. My isolation needed to die, the illusion that I could handle things alone. My pride and idealized self-image needed to die, as I began to face the darkness and confusion within me. And my shame needed to die, as I began to trust the love that would never desert me.

This will be terribly painful, but we ponder the cross of Christ not simply to watch a man die. We are here to die, too. What is it that needs to die so that the love that gave birth to us and that sustains us at every moment can break us open to resurrected life?

Maybe it is self-doubt, self-hatred, self-rejection that need to die, the debilitating conviction that we are not good enough, that we must prove our worth and earn God's favor. Maybe it's a relationship that needs to die or be radically transformed. Maybe it's some old pattern of behavior, some way of understanding who we are, that's been with us for as long as we can remember but that no longer serves life.

Jesus experienced total abandonment on the cross, for although God the Father in fact was with him, God the Son knew nothing about it. In the wilderness of our own desolation, we too, like Jesus, may have no felt awareness that God is near. Our prayer may be boring and dry, our heart heavy as a stone, our words empty, our mind distracted, desperate, or confused. God may seem impossibly far away, no more real than a mental construct or idle tale. Our longing for God may be intense because something crucial is breaking apart—we're in dire straits, we're going down— and only silence answers our entreaty and we feel no reassuring touch. As far as we know, we are abandoned and alone.

Yet even in the center of apparent abandonment, God *is* with us. God embraces the void. God doesn't take it away. God doesn't wipe it out. Instead, with an overflow of compassion, God shares the void with us. Like Jesus, we don't see God at all; all we know is the void. But the void is in God.

This is where trust comes in, radical trust. The old self that we think is our only self is falling apart. There may be nothing we can do but endure the process, letting our selves be dismantled and unmade while our birth awaits. We will feel utterly lost. But remembering the words of Jesus from the cross can give us hope. If we know that Christ entered and continues to enter human anguish and abandonment, then we know that our pain is not some private and meaningless crucifixion of our own. It is the crucifixion of Christ in which we share. We have entered Christ's abandonment, just as Christ has entered ours. The more completely we feel God's absence, the more fully we commune with Christ, and Christ with us. Our sense of abandonment thus becomes, paradoxically, the very place where we meet Christ. Loneliness becomes a place of encounter. When we feel bereft and cut off from God, we are intimately joined with Jesus, and he with us, although we do not feel his presence and must take this claim on faith.

Jesus' loneliest words from the cross weave us into a fabric of relationship with one another and with God that neither suffering nor death can destroy. His abandonment marks the end of ours. His question to God is actually a promise to us: even God's silence is filled with God.

We claim this promise for ourselves when we are willing to "take up our cross" and the spiritual discipline that goes with it. When we suffer and feel abandoned, we must take time to look and listen inwardly for Jesus. We must be willing to find a quiet, private place and to open ourselves to him. We must let ourselves feel our neediness and pain, our loneliness and fear, and let Christ be with us in whatever way he wants to be present to and with us.

We may become aware of him beside us or within us. If we sense his suffering, we may want to minister to him, for we know what it is to feel abandoned. If we sense his strength, we may want to ask for his help, for he knows our distress. Or we may not sense his presence at all and may need to wait patiently in the darkness, trusting that he is with us at a level that transcends image, thought, or feeling.

As we keep turning to Christ in our suffering, accepting the fact that he is with us even if we know nothing about it, we may find ourselves inspired and empowered to make necessary changes in our lives. We may be led to protest and stand up to personal, societal, or environmental injustice with a courage that we never knew we had.

As for the suffering that we are powerless to change, Jesus' companionship will help us persevere. Sometimes he will even give us the mysterious but vivid sense that we are sharing in his crucifixion and the new life that awaits beyond it. This conviction can bring a quiet sense of joy. It's not just that now we know that we do not suffer alone—we also sense that we are somehow sharing in Christ's redemptive work, that the pain we have been given to bear is our own small way of sharing in Christ's pain and thus in the salvation of the world. The author of Colossians knew this when he wrote, "I am now rejoicing in my sufferings for your sake, and in my flesh I am completing what is lacking in Christ's afflictions for the sake of his body, that is, the church" (Colossians 1:24).

Jesus' plaintive cry can give us to courage to die the death we need to die, trusting that God's hidden hands will carry us through.

To Ponder in Prayer . . .

Take some time to let Jesus draw close. Perhaps there is an image of Jesus that has particular power for you: The gentle one who welcomes children in his arms, the prophetic one who announces and calls into being a community of justice and peace, the compassionate one with power to heal, the suffering one who is not afraid of our pain, the risen one who shares his glory, or, as on the road to Emmaus (Luke 24:13–32), the one who comes in some unexpected form. Let your breath bring you an image of Christ. Take time to sense Jesus' presence with you.

If you have not yet integrated especially painful past events, you may want to undertake the following exercise in healing memories in the company of a trusted pastor, friend, or therapist. Spend time sensing Jesus' presence with you. Then recall a time in your life when you felt abandoned. Let a particular moment or scene become vivid. Where are you? How old are you? What are you wearing? What time of day is it? What do you see, smell, and hear?

Let Jesus enter the scene. What do you feel when he appears? Speak to him about what is going on. How does he respond? What does he do? Is there something he wants you to know? Is there something he wants to give you? What needs to happen? Let it happen.

When this feels complete, take time to thank him for any insights or gifts received. Let the scene fade and rest for a while in his presence.

1 Betty Jean Seymour, "The Risk of Incognito: Holy Week as an Occasion to Reflect upon the Hiddenness of God," *The Christian Century*, 15 April, 1981, p. 415.

2 *Last Letters from Stalingrad*, trans. Franz Schneider and Charles Gullans, (New York: New American Library, 1965). Quoted by Betty Jean Seymour, *ibid*.

FIVE

"I thirst."

(JOHN 19:28–29)

What an elemental cry. From the child who awakens in the middle of the night to ask for a glass of water to the Afghani farmer scratching at dry soil and praying for rain, human beings the world over rely on clean fresh water for their health and survival. Jesus' entreaty from the cross ripples through the pleas of billions of men, women, and children who lack safe drinking water or adequate sanitation. Around the world, waterways are drying up or dying of pollution. More than half of the United States has endured what is fast becoming one of the worst droughts in the last century. Crops are withering and wildfires spreading. Those in the so-called "developed" world are just beginning to understand how precious water is, and how much determination it will take to conserve and distribute the world's limited supply.

On the cross Jesus shares our basic need for water and for air. He is dying slowly in an agony of thirst and suffocation. He is weak. He is human. He is vulnerable. The one through whom all things were made, including rivers, lakes, seas, and oceans; the one with power to command the waves on the Sea of Galilee; the Good Shepherd who leads us beside the still waters and bears springs of living water within himself—this one has emptied himself utterly and now hangs thirsty on the cross.

Jesus' cry expresses not only physical thirst but also the deepest longing of the human soul. We may name our ultimate longing in different ways—perhaps as the search for happiness or meaning, as the yearning to be free, to love and be loved, or to find wisdom or inner peace—but however we name our deepest desire, it is fundamentally a longing for God. Created in the image of God, we've been given a thirst for God that only God can satisfy.

It may take us years, even a lifetime, to learn to listen to that deep desire and to follow where it leads. Jesus was well aware of the countless ways that human beings stifle or forget their fundamental longing for union with God. Much of his ministry, from his first words, "What are you looking for?" (John 1:38), to his last, "I thirst," addresses the question of desire. What do you really want? What will satisfy your deepest hunger and thirst?

How hard it can be to know and name our deepest need! Many of us have been socialized to pay no attention to what we want and not to take our desires seriously. Some of us were taught that good Christians aren't supposed to have desires, and that having needs is a sign of being selfish. A few of us become so exquisitely sensitive to those around us and so expert at anticipating and meeting other people's needs that we have no clue what we ourselves most want and are profoundly disconnected from our own passion and erotic energy.

Or maybe we want conflicting things, and our desires tug at us like the winds of St. Petersburg, which, according to Russian writer Nikolai Gogol, blow in every direction at once. Maybe we strive to desire nothing, since we've been disappointed one

too many times and want to stifle our longings for
fear of being hurt. Or maybe we're beset by cravings that seem bottomless, the insatiable, addictive
drive to buy more, eat more, drink more, do more.
Even if we don't have a full-blown addiction, until
we know what we most deeply want—until we are
able to claim our deepest thirst as a thirst for
God—we will be vulnerable to wanting things
simply because the culture around us says they are
desirable.

I remember the day I caught sight of a distant
truck emblazoned with big letters on its back door:
WHAT YOU'RE LOOKING FOR. Curious, I stepped on
the gas, and as I drew closer finally made out the
picture and the smaller print. A sultry young
woman was reclining in a chair, a cigarette dan-
gling between two fingers and a cloud of smoke en-
veloping her head. Ah. Now I knew what I was
supposed to need. The purpose of advertising is not
just to sell a particular product but to create a climate of craving in which human beings imagine
that our deepest identity is to be a consumer and
that our worth is measured by what we own. Turn
on the television, listen to the radio, or simply walk
down the street in any American city, and the mes-

sage is relentless: *You don't have enough. You can never have enough. You need what someone else has. You need more of what you already have.*

Jesus knew about our complex and troubled relationship to desire and how our deep longing for God can be hijacked or anesthetized. Jesus came to awaken our deepest desires and to set them free. "Ask, search, knock" (Matthew 7:7–11), he urged his followers, daring us to risk exploring and expressing our desires in prayer. Where have we shut our desires down, buried them, or let them fall asleep? Where have we let ourselves be distracted by trivialities or by the quest for something that will never fully satisfy? Have we begun to search for our own hidden treasure, the thing so precious that we joyfully relinquish everything else (Matthew 13:44–45)?

From beginning to end, Jesus was a man on fire with the love of God, and his fifth word from the cross focuses a lifetime of longing. His cry is the cry of every human soul that knows, in the well-known words of St. Augustine, that it will be restless until it finds its rest in God, and that without God it is "in a barren and dry land where there is no water" (Psalm 63:1).

But "I thirst" expresses not only humanity's longing for God. It also expresses God's desire for us. God longs for us even more than we long for God, and our very longing for God, our thirst for a genuine, heartfelt connection with the divine is itself a sign that God is stirring within us. On the cross, God gives up everything for us because words alone will not suffice. Through God's ultimate act of self-giving, God discloses that we are the pearl of great price. We are the treasure in the field, for whose sake everything else has been relinquished. To God we are infinitely desirable, however absurd, astonishing—or wondrous—that fact may seem.

Human and divine desiring meet in this word from the cross, as they do in every Eucharist. As we enter this energy field of love given and received, of mutual desires fully expressed, we will be moved to respond. Pondering Jesus hanging on the cross so dry, so parched, makes something in us surge forward, like the tide of some inward sea. We want to help him. We wish we could be the woman at the well (John 4:1–42) and give him something to drink. "I thirst," Jesus cries, and out of our stony heart flows a river of living water. Jesus' thirst awakens our own. So much of our compassion, so much of our longing for justice and peace springs from awareness of the thirsting Christ.

Mother Teresa, famous the world over for her ministry to the poor, was passionate about Jesus. A while before she died, she explained to a visitor in Calcutta that her mission to the poor and the dying was a way of showing her love for Jesus. "[People often] misunderstand us," Mother Teresa observed. "They think we do it first because we love the poor. Tell them we do it for Jesus. . . .We do it," she said, "with Jesus, for Jesus, and to Jesus."[1]

With Jesus, for Jesus, and to Jesus. How would our lives be changed if everything we did, from making our biggest decisions to carrying out the smallest, most mundane tasks of the day, were made with the awareness that we were doing these things with Jesus, for Jesus, and to Jesus? I don't mean just what we do in church—I mean all our ordinary actions, Monday through Saturday. If you did everything with Jesus, for Jesus, or to Jesus, would this change how you answer the phone, how you drive in traffic, even how you walk across a room? Would it affect the decisions you make, the words you speak, and your capacity to perceive the divine in even the most ordinary moments of the day? The only way to find out is to take up this spiritual discipline, practice it faithfully, and see what happens. One of the shortest paths to intimacy with God is to do everything in conscious relationship to Christ.

This is where joy comes in. It may be one of the best-kept secrets of the Christian life, but when you have a deep sense that God in Christ is longing for your love, and your response is yes, what comes up next is joy. For this is what we were made for. We were made for love, made to fall in love with the Source of life.

"I thirst for you," says God. "I long for you. Will you turn to me? Will you say yes?"

God is so vulnerable sometimes. We're all vulnerable when we ask for love, since love can't be forced—it can only be freely given. And never is God's longing so straightforward, so direct, as when we see God on the cross, pouring out God's self for our sake.

To Ponder in Prayer . . .

Listen to Jesus as he says, "I thirst." Do his words express your desire for God? Quietly repeat the words, if doing so helps you express your longing. You may wish to find your own words or to let the words fall away. Stay with the desire for God as long as you can. How does God respond?

Continue listening to Jesus. His words express God's longing for you. Stay with this awareness of God's love for you as long as you can. How do you respond?

Jesus takes your desires seriously. His first words to those who approach him in the Gospel according to John are "What do you seek? What are you looking for?" Take some time to imagine that Jesus is asking you this question. What is your response?

Where are your buried desires? Where has disappointment, resignation, or cynicism closed you down? Are there longings you've never dared to explore, perhaps because you didn't feel your desires were worth a hearing or that you were not worth being listened to? Talk to Jesus about your desires. What does Jesus desire for you?

Choose a simple, routine activity (for example, preparing or eating a meal, washing dishes, or making a bed) and give that activity your complete and loving attention. Be aware of every sensation—

the colors and smells of the food, the warmth of the water, the weight of the sheets. Take your time. There's no hurry. Imagine that you are doing this simple activity in the presence of Jesus. Perhaps you are doing it with Jesus, or for Jesus, or to Jesus.

How does this practice effect your awareness of the divine? How does it effect your attitude to life? Do you notice an increased capacity to pay attention in each moment or a deeper sense of gratitude? How does this practice contrast with your usual approach to routine activities?

1 Quoted by Ed Bauman, *Ministry of Money* newsletter, December, 1993. Ministry of Money provides retreats, programs, and "pilgrimages of reverse mission" to help participants explore their relationship to money from a faith perspective (http://www.ministryofmoney.org)

SIX

"It is finished."

(JOHN 19:30)

At this moment just before his death, Jesus knows that his work and his life are complete. He has fulfilled what he was sent here to do.

Jesus was clear about his mission. "I have come that they may have life," he said, "and have it abundantly" (John 10:10). Everything he did—teaching, preaching, provoking, consoling, healing—sprang from that single purpose, that deep commitment. His eyes were fixed on the reign of God, and nothing could stop him: not the opinions of other people, not praise, not blame, not the cross, not death.

Jesus had found true north on his own inner compass. He had discovered his heart's desire, something big enough to live for and big enough to die for. Yes, he was sometimes afraid. Yes, the cost was total. But he had discovered his own deepest desiring, the passion for God that made him willing to do anything, even to die, in order to express the longing of his heart.

In times like ours the thought of living so passionately for God may sound horrifying. Who lives passionately for God? Religious fanatics. Christian fundamentalists who stalk and bomb abortion clinics. Middle Eastern terrorists who strap explosives to their chests and walk into a busy marketplace or board a crowded bus. Muslim extremists who smash commercial jetliners into office buildings in the name of Allah. If living passionately for God means condoning religious violence—an equation that Christianity has made too many times in the course of its own bloody history, especially in its history of anti-Semitism—then we must condemn it.

But what does it mean to live passionately for God? Our answer depends entirely on our understanding of who God is and what sorts of things please God. Jesus calls us not only to love God with our whole heart, soul, mind, and strength, but also to love our neighbors as ourselves (Mark 12:29–31). This is hardly a summons to the hatred, fear, and self-righteousness that pour from the mouths of fanatics.

Jesus lived passionately for God. He surrendered his autonomous self-will, listened deeply for what the Spirit moved him to do and then did it. But he was no fundamentalist or fanatic. He didn't live by a fixed set of rules, beliefs, and habits. Instead, he lived spontaneously, often outside of conventional norms, by the Spirit of love rather than the judgmental letter of the law. He crossed boundaries and reached out to the rejected and forgotten. He blessed and socialized with people living at the margins. Jesus offered freedom, a freedom that was and is larger, more creative, and more imbued with mystery than anything that religious fanatics (and many of today's secularists) can possibly know.

Like Jesus, we Christians may also long to give ourselves to God completely. Even when we are aware of life's inevitable ironies, paradoxes, and contradictions, we yearn for something that transcends them. I wonder if our aversion to be-coming a "religious fanatic" sometimes conceals an almost wistful yearning to find something to which we can wholeheartedly belong and to which we can give ourselves completely, a longing to sur-render ourselves to a Love that will never let us go. If we have little sense of our life's purpose, if we don't believe that we matter to God or don't feel that our lives are expressing our deepest values and commitments, then we will find ourselves living without zest or zing. Simple tasks will weigh on us like a burden, mere chores to cross off the list of things to do. We will struggle with bore-dom, distraction, and irritable resentment, fending off a nagging sense that the grand adventure of life has somehow passed us by.

Each of us faces the same question that Jesus faced: What have I been sent here to do? What is the dream that wants to become realized in my life? What makes my heart sing? What is it, deep down, that I truly want my life to express? How can I bear witness to what I value most? Where do I find my deepest joy?

The first answers that come to mind may be those supplied by the ego or our consumer culture, both of which conspire to kidnap our vocation and turn it into a matter of personal ambition. We know what that's like: the itch for fame, money, power, glory. We know the drill: *Grab everything you can. Prove your worth. Get to the top. Make your mark. Be a success. See your name in lights.*

But we don't have to settle for what the ego wants; its cravings never satisfy the longings of the soul. The heftiest portfolio or the sleekest body, the widest name recognition or the most fashionable address, the most impressive resume or the longest obituary—these trophies of a consumer culture do not entice the soul. The path of Christ moves beyond that level of discourse, beckoning us into a larger, riskier, and more glorious project than self-promotion and image-management. Christ calls us to be transformed: to live not for ourselves alone, but for him, for one another, for this good earth, for all God's creation. Finding our true vocation is de-centering to the ego. It's the discovery of a deeper wanting than what the self-glorifying autonomous ego wants. It's the discovery of a joy that goes beyond self-gratification: the desire to seek and find a way to serve.

Frederich Buechner once said, "The place God

calls you to is the place where your deep gladness and the world's deep hunger meet."[1] When we find that intersection, that meeting-place between our joy and the world's hunger, we make the electrifying discovery, "*This* is what I was made for. *This* is what my life is about." In a way it's not about us at all.

Olympic gold medalist Eric Liddell knew that. Perhaps you've seen the movie *Chariots of Fire*. It's the story of the Scottish runner who set a world record in the 400-yard dash at the 1924 Olympics. After winning a gold medal, Eric Liddell traveled to China, was ordained a minister, became a missionary, and eventually died in a Japanese prison camp. Liddell attributed his Olympic win to God, and once commented, "When I run, I feel God's pleasure."

Where do *you* feel God's pleasure? In what situations do you feel most fully alive, most authentically yourself? What is the place of your deepest joy? Your answer may be a clue to your vocation, evidence of the way that God is inviting you to participate in restoring all people to unity with God and each other in Christ. For it was joy that pulled Jesus forward, joy that led him to run with perseverance the race that was set before him, even when it led to the cross (Hebrews 12:1b–2). We don't have to be Olympic runners, but we who have been baptized into Christ *do* need to find our deepest joy and to run the race that is set before us, seeking in everything we do to love and serve God "with gladness and singleness of heart."[2]

Unless we know what we've come here to do, why we've been placed on this earth, we won't be able to say at the end of our lives, with the author of Second Timothy, "I have fought the good fight, I have finished the race, I have kept the faith" (4:7). We won't be able to say, with Jesus, "It is finished."

I hear in Jesus' words a challenge to each of us to ask the Holy Spirit to show us what we most deeply desire and what we have been sent here to do. I also hear something else: a challenge to accept the limits of what we can accomplish. We all have a part to play in the drama of salvation, but it is not we who complete that salvation. It is God in Christ, through the power of the Spirit.

That's a truth that I, like many activists, can find it difficult to accept. Over the last few years I've felt a deepening call to work for environmental justice and the healing of our relationship not just

to our own bodies but to the larger "body" of the
Earth. I've found deep satisfaction in this growing
passion, but I've also had to learn humility. As I
gaze at the cross, one thing that needs to die in me
is my reliance on myself and on human effort
alone. Yes, I want to galvanize everyone to care
about the Earth and to work to restore its wholeness. Yes, I want to turn this ship around before it
crashes into the iceberg, or, to change the metaphor
since we humans are making the icebergs melt, I
want to turn this ship around before we find ourselves floating aimlessly on high new seas. I do not
want our children to be born into a world of dying
waters full of whale carcasses, dead coral reefs, and
oil slicks, with a hot sun burning relentlessly over-
head. Yes, I want to do everything I can.

But if I try to do this work alone, if I try to
"make my mark" without relying on the grace
and power of God, then my work quickly becomes just another project of the ego and I quickly
burn out, as have so many activists before me. If I
don't keep my eyes steadily fixed on God and the
vision of God's reign that beckons me forward
like a prize, then my hopes rise and fall with every
immediate success and failure. I might as well be

a weekend warrior who mistook the Boston Marathon for a sprint.

I need to rest in the power of the cross. I need to admit that I myself can't save the world, only Jesus can—and *that* he can, and does, and has. When I listen to Jesus say "It is finished," I have a chance to release the tension and to let go of the anxious rush to make a difference, to do it *all*, to do it *now*, to do it *myself*, to do it *perfectly*. I can breathe in the power of the cross, the love that meets us not only in our suffering, but also in our longing for justice and healing. I can breathe in the love and receive Christ's strength for the journey ahead.

To Ponder in Prayer . . .

Let your breath bring you images of times when you felt most fully alive, most fully yourself. When in your life have you felt most connected to your deepest love? In what kinds of situations do you feel most fully engaged with life? What sorts of moments bring you joy?

Imagine that when you were conceived and born, you were sent to earth on a mission. What were you sent here to do? What were you sent here to give? To receive? To learn?

If you were on your deathbed, looking back over your life, how would you hope that the world had been blessed by your having been here? What needs to happen so that, with Jesus, you too can say, "It is finished"? What happens in you now as you let yourself rest in the power of Jesus' cross and trust in the great work that he has already done?

1 Frederick Buechner, *Wishful Thinking: A Seeker's ABC*, revised and expanded ed. (HarperSanFrancisco, 1993), p. 119.

2 Post-Communion Prayer, *The Book of Common Prayer*, (New York: Church Publishing, Inc., 1979), p. 365.

SEVEN

"Father, into your hands
I commend my spirit."

(LUKE 23:46–49)

I remember an October afternoon a few years back. It was a golden day, full of wind and sunshine, and as the maple trees tossed their branches in the air, cascades of leaves fell all around. The leaves were tumbling through the air, and I had the odd impression that the trees were willingly, even exuberantly, letting them go. All those leaves that had begun in the spring as tiny buds holding tight to the branch, unfurling and maturing over the summer into a rich dark green, and then blazing into gold and red in the fall—the time had come to let them go. And so at last the trees released them into the wind, holding nothing back. Nothing holding anything anywhere.

I thought to myself: I'd like to die like that. I'd like to live like that. I'd like to live and die with that kind of openhearted abandon, that complete generosity of spirit.

That is what I hear in this seventh and final word of Christ from the cross: a word of trust, of complete self-giving. "Father, into your hands I commend my spirit." Jesus is quoting a verse from Psalm 31, a verse, I'm told, that every Jewish mother taught her child to pray at bedtime. Just as many of us were taught to pray "Now I lay me down to sleep," so a Jewish mother would teach her child to pray "Into your hands I commend my spirit." To these words Jesus adds "Father." Even on a cross, Jesus relinquishes his life with the trust of a child falling asleep in his father's or mother's arms.[1]

Sometimes the only way to grow into our full stature in Christ (Ephesians 4:11–16) is to hold fast, to exert ourselves, to do everything in our power to bring something into being or to make something happen. A glance through the Bible reveals many passages that enjoin us to hold on and hold fast. "Let your heart hold fast my words; keep my commandments, and live" (Proverbs 4:4); "Hold fast to love and justice" (Hosea 12:6); "Hold fast to what is good" (Romans 12:9); "Let us hold fast to our confession" (Hebrews 4:14). Jesus likewise urged his followers to keep his commandments (e.g. John 15:10) and act upon his words (e.g. Matthew 7:24). Christianity is in some ways a very "muscular" religion in which we hear an energizing summons to exercise our will, to be active, and to hold fast.

But if learning to hold on is essential to growing up in Christ, so is learning to let go. "Drop your nets," Jesus tells us (see Matthew 4:19–20). "Take no gold, or silver, or copper in your belts, no bag for your journey" (Matthew 10:9–10). "Leave family and possessions behind" (see Matthew 10:37 and 6:19). "Come with me on a search for what is of utmost value, and let everything else go" (see Matthew 13:44–45).

Becoming our true selves in Christ depends on learning when (and to what) to hold on and when (and what) to let go. Just as a musician learns when to sustain a note and when to let it dissolve into silence, and just as a dancer learns when to hold a muscle's tension and when to release it, so in our spiritual lives we must learn the difficult art of embrace and release.

What does God ask us to let go? The answer is different for each of us. We may need to let go our self-doubt and self-hatred. We may need to let go perfectionism, the anxious attempt to get it "right," or the incessant urge to please other people. We may need to let go of our attachment to looking good and to protecting and polishing our image. We may need to relinquish a habit of worry, or our frantic clutching at alcohol, food, work, nicotine, or sex. We may need to drop our cynicism, or let bitterness and self-pity fall away. We may need to give up our quest for fame, wealth, or power. It's not that all these things are necessarily bad in themselves, but when they become our ultimate value, they become demonic and crowd Love out.

Learning to love God first provokes a repeated crisis of value. Again and again we discover that the only way to "hold fast" to Christ is to face the painful—though ultimately freeing—process of letting other things go. And in the end, of course, we do have to let everything go. Our various achievements, the trophies that line the shelves, the books

we've written, the battles we've won, the possessions we've collected—all these will be taken from
us at the moment of death. In that radical self-emp-
tying we will have to let go everything we've been
clinging to and everything we've known—our
loved ones, our good (or bad) judgments of ourselves, our memories, our bodies—and open ourselves entirely to the grace of God.

Will this be a moment of trust and self-giving?
Will we be able to say, "Father, into your hands I
commend my spirit"? Such a response can't be
willed or forced. In some sense it is a gift, this capacity to trust that God is present even if we know
nothing about it. But we long for that kind of
serenity, the inner peace that comes whenever we
surrender control and give ourselves in faith to the
Holy Mystery who breathes life into us and receives
our spirit when we die.

What would it be like to live and die like a leaf
that throws itself joyfully into the wind of God?
Can we learn to die (and to live) as Jesus did, offering our spirit to God and holding nothing back?
We can begin right here, with our own breath. The
ancient Hebrews believed that our breath is our
life. If we live, it is because God keeps putting

God's breath or "spirit" into us. Breath by breath, moment by moment, it is the presence of God that keeps us alive[2]. Every breath thus gives us an opportunity to practice breathing in God's Spirit and releasing it back to God. Our breath can teach us to let go.

So can our dreams. Several years ago a dream came to me that has returned in one form or another a number of times since. I suppose the dream will keep visiting me until I have finally absorbed what it has to say. I tell it in the third person since it is one of those dreams that doesn't seem just for me, but for the "tribe," the whole community. Perhaps it will offer you a glimpse into what Jesus was experiencing as he spoke his last words and released his last breath.

One night a woman dreamed that she was coming to the end of a long journey with many other people. After many adventures and trials, they had finally reached the top of a mountain. In front of them stretched an abyss. Across the abyss they saw a teacher, a holy man, sitting on a ledge beside a doorway filled with golden light. The seekers understood that they were welcome to enter the doorway if they walked across the abyss.

They talked this over among themselves. They shrugged. They laughed. "No way!" they said to each other. "Forget it! You've got to be kidding!"

But the woman decided to try. "If I don't try," she said, "then all my life up to this moment will have no meaning." Instantly, beautiful, sentimental music began to play. Everyone praised her for her heroism and courage, and she felt pleased with herself.

But she also started to see what it was that she would have to let go, including, most clearly, not only where she'd been wounded or hurt, but also where she'd been healed. She would have to let go both the suffering and the healing that she'd experienced in her life. This seemed very hard to do, but she took courage from the sentimental music, and the sense of drama and self-conscious heroism that it gave her.

"This won't be so bad," she said to herself.

"Stop the music!" said the Teacher. "You must cross in silence."

The only words she could speak were these: "Lord, have mercy. Christ, have mercy." And just as she was about to begin to walk across the abyss, the Teacher made the golden door disappear. So now she had to walk across the abyss toward a blank wall.

She began to walk, repeating "Lord, have mercy. Christ, have mercy," stepping into thin air. She was walking on nothing, yet her feet were supported and she did not fall. She crossed the abyss. She reached the wall. But the doorway did not reappear. "This is harder than I thought!" she said to herself.

For a moment she was afraid. Maybe she'd been a fool to trust the Teacher. Maybe she'd been a fool to trust anyone with her life. And then, in some silent, secret place within herself, she let go. She surrendered to Christ completely.

The doorway opened, and she stepped through, into golden light.

To Ponder in Prayer . . .

Find a comfortable position in which you can be both relaxed and alert. Close your eyes. Take a few deep breaths to release any tension in your body. Then let the breath return to its normal rhythm. Become aware of the air as it moves in and out of your nostrils. Try not to control your breathing.

Let the breath come and go as it pleases. Feel the touch of the air as it passes through your nostrils. Is it warm or cool? In what part of the nostrils do you feel the air as you exhale? Be alert to the slightest hint of air on your nostrils as you inhale and exhale.

As you breathe in, understand that it is God who is breathing into you. Draw in God's Spirit with every breath. The air you are breathing is charged with the power and the presence of God. As you draw air into your lungs, you are drawing God in. As you breathe out, relax into God's presence. Let each breath deepen your awareness of the nearness of God, breathing into you, breathing through you. Be as aware of each breath as if it were your first breath—or your last. This is the breath that God is giving you.

If it helps to focus your awareness on God, try saying inwardly with each breath in, "I come from You," and with each breath out, "I return to You."

Another variation is to pray "Loving Mother, Father, into your hands I commend my spirit." Let the prayer become very simple, maybe just a few words silently repeated in rhythm with the breath (e.g., "Into your hands" on the in-breath, "I give

my spirit" on the out-breath, or even "your hands
. . . my spirit").

1 William Barclay, *The Gospel of Luke*, rev. ed.
(Philadelphia: The Westminster Press, 1975), p. 288.

2 For these remarks about the breath and for part of the
closing meditation, I am indebted to Anthony de Mello,
S.J.'s classic book of meditations, *Sadhana, a Way to
God: Christian Exercises in Eastern Form*, (Poona,
India, 1978; New York: Doubleday, 1984), "God in My
Breath," pp. 36–37.

COWLEY PUBLICATIONS is a ministry of the Society of Saint John the Evangelist, a religious community of men in the Episcopal Church. Emerging from the Society's tradition of prayer, theological reflection, and diversity of mission, the press is centered in the rich heritage of the Anglican Communion.

Cowley Publications seeks to provide books, audio cassettes, CDs, and other resources for the ongoing theological exploration and spiritual development of the Episcopal Church and others in the body of Christ. To this end, it is dedicated to developing a new generation of theological writers, encouraging them to produce timely, creative, and stimulating publications of excellence, and making these publications available widely, reaching both clergy and lay persons.